SRI LANKA

...in Pictures

Visual Geography Series®

SRI LANKA

...in Pictures

Prepared by
Geography Department

Lerner Publications Company
Minneapolis

Independent Picture Service

Using a graceful movement, a Sri Lankan farmer sows seeds by hand.

This is an all-new edition of the Visual Geography Series. Previous editions have been published by Sterling Publishing Company, New York City, and some of the original textual information has been retained. New photographs, maps, charts, captions, and updated information have been added. The text has been entirely reset in 10/12 Century Textbook.

LIBRARY OF CONGRESS CATALOGING-IN-PUBLICATION DATA

Sri Lanka in pictures / prepared by Geography
Department.
    p. cm. — (Visual geography series)
    Includes index.
    Summary: Sri Lanka's topography, history, society,
economy, and government are concisely described, augmented by photographs, maps, charts, and captions.
    ISBN 0-8225-1853-8
    1. Sri Lanka. [1. Sri Lanka.] I. Lerner Publications
Company. Geography Dept. II. Series: Visual geography series (Minneapolis, Minn.).
DS489.S734 1989
954.9'3—dc19   88-15888
                                        CIP
                                        AC

International Standard Book Number: 0-8225-1853-8
Library of Congress Card Catalog Number: 88-15888

VISUAL GEOGRAPHY SERIES®

Publisher
Harry Jonas Lerner
Associate Publisher
Nancy M. Campbell
Senior Editor
Mary M. Rodgers
Editor
Gretchen Bratvold
Assistant Editors
Dan Filbin
Kathleen S. Heidel
Illustrations Editor
Karen A. Sirvaitis
Consultants/Contributors
Patrick Mendis
Sandra K. Davis
Designer
Jim Simondet
Cartographer
Carol F. Barrett
Indexer
Kristine S. Schubert
Production Manager
Richard J. Hannah

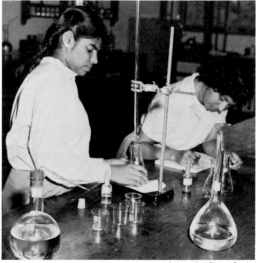

Independent Picture Service

Two Sri Lankan students record data as part of a high school chemistry course.

Acknowledgments

Title page photo by Drs. A. A. M. van der Heyden, Naarden, the Netherlands.

Elevation contours adapted from *The Times Atlas of the World*, seventh comprehensive edition (New York: Times Books, 1985).

1 2 3 4 5 6 7 8 9 10 98 97 96 95 94 93 92 91 90 89

Independent Picture Service

Devout Buddhists—followers of the religion founded in northern India by the philosopher Gautama Buddha in the sixth century B.C.—climb the Rock of Mihintale, where missionaries first preached the Buddhist faith in Sri Lanka.

Contents

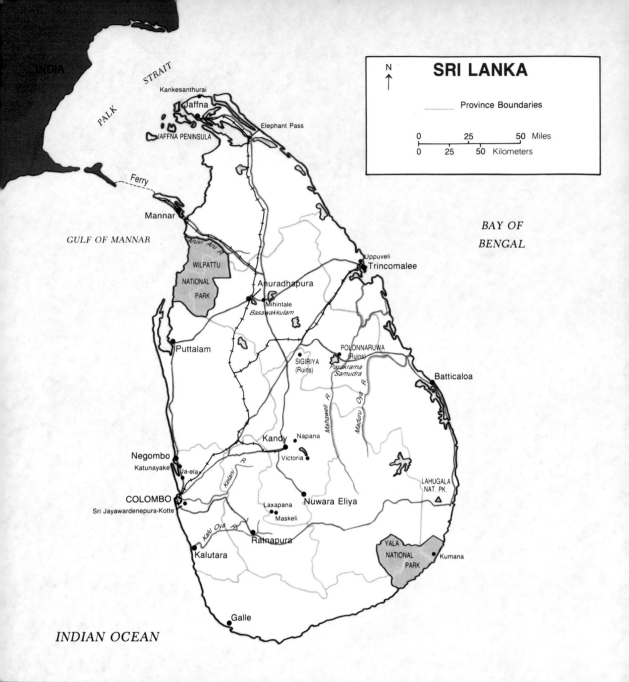

INDIA

PALK STRAIT

Kankesanthurai
Jaffna
JAFFNA PENINSULA
Elephant Pass

PALK

Ferry

Mannar

GULF OF MANNAR

BAY OF
BENGAL

N

SRI LANKA

Province Boundaries

0   25   50   Miles
0   25   50   Kilometers

Aruvi Aru R.
WILPATTU
NATIONAL
PARK

Uppuveli
Trincomalee

Anuradhapura
Mihintale
Basawakkulam

Puttalam

POLONNARUWA
(Ruins)

SIGIRIYA
(Ruins)
Parakrama
Samudra

Batticaloa

Mahaweli R.
Maduru Oya R.

Kandy   Napana

Victoria

Negombo
Katunayake   Ua-ela

Kelani R.

LAHUGALA
NAT. PK.

COLOMBO
Sri Jayawardenepura-Kotte

Laxapana
Maskeli

Nuwara Eliya

Kalu Oya

Ratnapura

YALA
NATIONAL
PARK

Kumana

Kalutara

Galle

INDIAN OCEAN

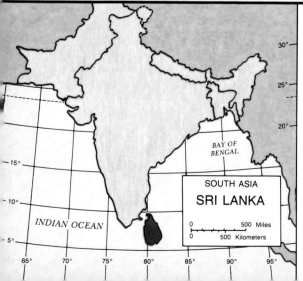

BAY OF
BENGAL

30°

25°

20°

15°

SOUTH ASIA

SRI LANKA

10°

INDIAN OCEAN

5°

0   500   Miles
0   500   Kilometers

65°   70°   75°   80°   85°   90°   95°

METRIC CONVERSION CHART
To Find Approximate Equivalents

WHEN YOU KNOW:	MULTIPLY BY:	TO FIND:
AREA		
acres	0.41	hectares
square miles	2.59	square kilometers
CAPACITY		
gallons	3.79	liters
LENGTH		
feet	30.48	centimeters
yards	0.91	meters
miles	1.61	kilometers
MASS (weight)		
pounds	0.45	kilograms
tons	0.91	metric tons
VOLUME		
cubic yards	0.77	cubic meters
TEMPERATURE		
degrees Fahrenheit	0.56 (after subtracting 32)	degrees Celsius

A dancer from the Kandy *perahera,* an annual Buddhist festival, keeps alive some of the island's ancient traditions.

Introduction

Sri Lanka, known as Ceylon until 1972, is an island republic situated in the Indian Ocean near the southeastern tip of India. Because of its strategic location, Sri Lanka has attracted traders, conquerors, and colonizers from the Middle East, eastern Asia, and Europe throughout its history. Nevertheless, a strong local culture has thrived, absorbing cultural elements from the Arabs, Chinese, Portuguese, Dutch, and British who came to the island. As a result, Sri Lanka's population is a mixture—mainly of Sinhalese people, who are the descendants of northern Indians, and the Tamil, whose roots lie in southern India. The island also is home to Muslims, whose ancestors were Arab merchants; Malays, from what is now Malaysia; and people of European ancestry.

These diverse groups have often disagreed about how Sri Lanka should develop as a nation. After the island achieved independence from Britain in 1948, disputes occurred mostly between the Tamil minority and the Sinhalese majority. Because they see themselves at a political and cultural disadvantage in Sri Lanka, Tamil militants have sought to establish a separate Tamil state in Sri Lanka's northern and eastern provinces. The Sri Lankan government has refused to allow such a state to exist.

From this conflict a Tamil guerrilla movement has emerged. The movement's members have engaged in terrorist activities, killing and injuring both civilians and government troops. In response, Sri Lankan soldiers have attacked Tamil villages. The government of India—whose own Tamil population supports the rebels —has helped Sri Lanka try to persuade the Sri Lankan Tamil to lay down their weapons. The violence, however, continues to claim Sri Lankan lives and to leave thousands of people homeless.

Although civil strife decreases foreign investments and tourism—two sources of income that Sri Lanka cannot afford to lose—a strong plantation economy produces most of the nation's revenue. Continued agricultural growth is tied to the government's ability to stabilize the country's internal conflicts. Sri Lanka's economic and political future, therefore, depends on its people finding a solution that will satisfy the island's ethnic groups.

Photo by Ruthi Soudack

Sri Lanka's economy heavily depends on its agricultural output. Here, women in Napana gather and bind stalks of rice.

A long avenue bordered by royal palms is a feature of the Peradeniya Botanical Gardens – once a park for Sri Lankan kings – in the central highlands.

1) The Land

Covering 25,332 square miles in the Indian Ocean, the island of Sri Lanka is separated from the Asian subcontinent of India by the Gulf of Mannar and the Palk Strait. Sri Lanka's greatest length is 270 miles from north to south, and its greatest width is 140 miles from west to east. To the east of Sri Lanka is the Bay of Bengal, which stretches from India to Burma. In area, the nation is slightly larger than the state of West Virginia and includes several small islands off its northern and north-western coasts in its territory.

Topography

Sri Lanka has two main landscape features. Coastal lowlands encircle the island, blending inland with plains in the north, south, and east; and a section of highlands

9

Most of Sri Lanka's coastal areas lie in the dry zone, so called because it receives less rainfall than the central highlands, or wet zone.

Courtesy of Patrick Mendis

covers much of the southwestern and central provinces. These two regions are also characterized by the differing amounts of seasonal rainfall they each receive. Thus the coastal lowlands and inland areas—with their relatively low precipitation levels—are called the dry zone, and the moist highlands are known as the wet zone.

THE DRY ZONE

The dry zone extends over four-fifths of the island's territory. This zone contains most of the coastal belt, which rises from sea level to 100 feet and is 25 miles across at its widest point. Irregularly indented with inlets and lagoons, the coast features sandy beaches and offshore coral reefs.

Stretching between 5 and 25 miles inland from the coast are rolling plains that encompass the major portion of Sri Lanka's territory. Although the region is generally low and flat, occasional hills—actually underground masses of granite that have pushed through the earth—break up the

By producing abundant tea harvests, the fertile soil of the wet zone supports much of Sri Lanka's export economy.

Photo by Drs. A. A. M. van der Heyden, Naarden, the Netherlands

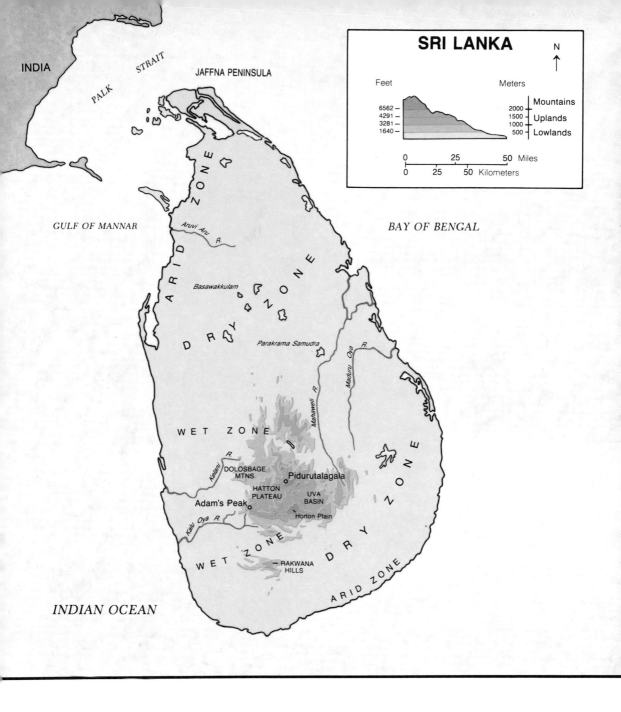

SRI LANKA

N ↑

Feet		Meters	
		2000	Mountains
6562 —		1500	Uplands
4291 —		1000	
3281 —		500	Lowlands
1640 —			

0   25   50 Miles
0   25   50 Kilometers

INDIA

PALK STRAIT

JAFFNA PENINSULA

GULF OF MANNAR

BAY OF BENGAL

ARID ZONE

Aruvi Aru R.

Basawakkulam

DRY ZONE

Parakrama Samudra

Maduru Oya R.

Mahaweli R.

WET ZONE

Kelani R.

DOLOSBAGE MTNS.

Pidurutalagala

HATTON PLATEAU

UVA BASIN

Adam's Peak

Horton Plain

Kalu Oya R.

DRY ZONE

WET ZONE

RAKWANA HILLS

ARID ZONE

INDIAN OCEAN

landscape. The soil in the region is made up of loose stone and eroded rock, except for the northern Jaffna Peninsula, which consists of limestone.

THE WET ZONE

The plains gradually rise in elevation in south central Sri Lanka to form a region of peaks that vary from 3,000 to over 8,000 feet in height. Narrow ravines, deep valleys, and high plateaus interrupt the highland landscape, which covers the remaining one-fifth of Sri Lanka's territory.

A long, central ridge within the highlands features Pidurutalagala, the nation's highest peak at 8,281 feet above sea level. Nearby are the high, fertile plains of Nuwara Eliya and Horton, where tea plants

The Mahaweli River – called the Mahaveli-ganga in Sri Lanka – flows northeast through the central highlands and empties into the Bay of Bengal at Trincomalee.

thrive. Plateaus, such as Hatton Plateau to the west and the Uva Basin to the east, flank the central ridge. The western plateau contains Adam's Peak (7,360 feet), which for centuries has been a place of religious pilgrimage for people of the Buddhist, Islamic, and Christian faiths. Other uplands—including the Rakwana Hills and the Dolosbage Mountains—lie south and northwest of the central ridge.

Rivers and Lakes

Most of Sri Lanka's rivers begin in the highlands and travel over steep waterfalls before flowing through the inland plains to the Indian Ocean. The rivers are too short and too rapid to serve as sea-lanes, but the waterways have great potential as sources of hydroelectric power.

Of the nation's 16 major waterways, the Mahaweli River is the longest and flows for 206 miles through the dry zone to Trincomalee on the northeastern coast. In the 1980s the government started a program to develop the Mahaweli as a source of hydroelectric power and irrigation for the

dry zone. The Kelani River ends near Colombo, the capital city, on the west coast. The Kalu Oya River reaches the Indian Ocean near Kalutara on the southwest

Early Sri Lankan kings built huge reservoirs, called tanks, to irrigate dry areas of the island.

coast, and the Aruvi Aru flows northwest across the dry zone to Mannar.

The rivers effectively irrigate and drain the highlands because the waterways flow swiftly downward to their sea outlets. In contrast, on the plain and along the coast—where the terrain is level—water sometimes collects and floods settlements, roads, and farmland. As a result, homes and overland routes in these regions usually lie far from the riverbanks.

Although Sri Lanka contains few lakes, it does have a number of artificial reservoirs, known as tanks, some of which are over 2,000 years old. The oldest of these tanks is Basawakkulam, which was constructed in 300 B.C. to collect and store water for the ancient city of Anuradhapura in north central Sri Lanka.

Courtesy of Patrick Mendis

Pepper vines thrive in the moist soil of Sri Lanka's hill country.

Courtesy of Ceylon Tourist Board, Colombo

Waterfalls, such as this one near Badulla, frequently interrupt the course of rivers in the highlands.

Flora and Fauna

The vegetation of Sri Lanka reflects the island's climate pattern and topography. Thus the well-watered regions of the central highlands and of the southwestern coast are lush with vegetation, and evergreen rain-forests are common. Hundreds of species of flowering shrubs—including hibiscus, frangipani, bougainvillea, tree ferns, and orchids—are found along with groves of mango, cinnamon, cacao, and banana trees. Rubber plantations lie between the highland tea estates and the coastal coconut plantations.

The elevated plateaus have limited areas of coarse grass, called patanas, in addition to forests and thick jungles. The wet patanas cover Horton Plains and the area around Nuwara Eliya, and the dry patanas grow especially well in the Uva Basin.

In the southwestern lowlands, many varieties of palm trees—including areca and coconut—thrive. Mangroves and pandanus trees grow well in coastal areas. Trees used for lumber, such as mahogany, are native to the wet zone, and acacias, eucalypti, and cypresses also grow in various parts of the region.

13

Mahouts—keepers and riders of elephants—take great care of their animals, including bathing them daily. Elephants are protected under Sri Lanka's strict wildlife preservation laws.

In the dry zone, fertile soil and long-established systems of irrigation keep the countryside green. Much of the dry zone has scrub vegetation and forests that include ebony, satinwood, and several other valuable trees. The eastern region features a few grassland areas, called *talawas*. In these regions, however, desert conditions can arise if monsoon rains fail to appear.

Sri Lanka is famous for the variety of its wildlife, which is protected by law. Along with elephants, larger wild animals include bears, wild boars, leopards, cheetahs, deer, and buffalo. Several wildlife reserves—including Yala and Wilpattu national parks—preserve the natural habitats of the nation's animals.

A sanctuary at Kumana on the southeastern coast protects birds, who are able to live in safety from human and animal hunters. Peacocks are native to the island, and scientists have counted members of over 350 other species of birdlife on the island.

The government has declared the sea around the southern coral reef a preserve for Sri Lanka's many beautiful fish—including sturgeons, Moorish idols, and butterfly fish. In unprotected waters, fishermen catch sailfish, sharks, pompano, marlins, groupers, barracuda, and horse mackerel.

Climate

Because of its location near the equator, Sri Lanka has a tropical climate, with temperatures that remain between 60° and 90° F throughout the year. Sea breezes moderate lowland temperatures, and high altitudes cool the mountainous areas. The coastal city of Colombo averages 77° F in January and 82° F in May. Mountainous Nuwara Eliya, on the other hand, records temperatures of 57° F and 60° F in the same two months.

The wet zone in the southwestern part of Sri Lanka benefits from the southwest monsoon, a seasonal wind that occurs between May and November and that carries heavy rainfall—sometimes as much as 200 inches. Precipitation levels in the wet zone usually average more than 100 inches per year, however.

The dry zone in the northeastern region receives the northeast monsoon, which arrives from the Bay of Bengal between December and February. Annual rainfall in the dry zone is between 50 and 75 inches, and most crops in the northern and eastern lowlands require irrigation. Two relatively arid zones along the southeastern and northwestern coasts get between 25 and 50 inches of rainfall each year.

Drought and flooding are common problems in Sri Lanka, due to deforestation and land erosion. During the two periods between the monsoons, thunderstorms are more frequent in the wet zone than in the dry zone.

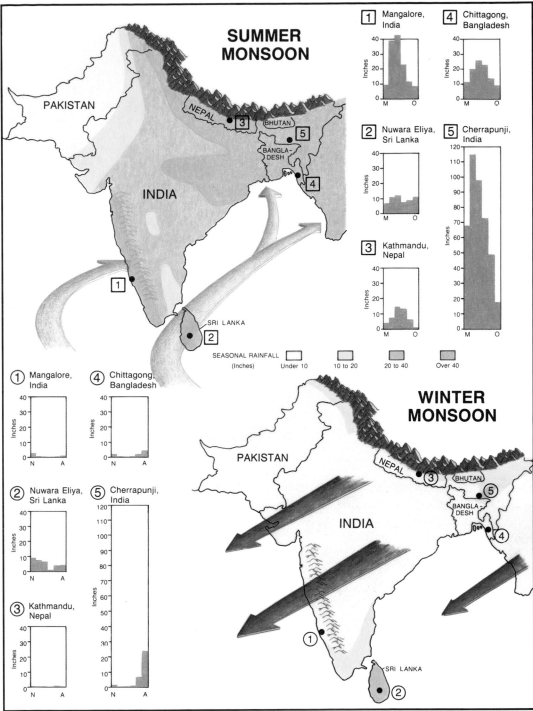

These maps show the seasonal shift of winds, called monsoons, over southern Asia and the rainfall levels for five cities in the region. In summer (May to October), the monsoon winds blow from sea to land, carrying moisture—which is released as rain—as they pass over this part of the Asian continent. In winter (November to April), the monsoons blow from land to sea. Because they originate over a cold, arid land surface, the winter winds are dry, and little or no rainfall is associated with them. Nuwara Eliya, Sri Lanka, differs from the other places shown on the maps. This city's winter winds are rain-bearing because they pass over the Bay of Bengal before hitting the island. Similar to the rest of the region, however, Nuwara Eliya's heaviest rains come in the summer. Climate data taken from *World-Climates* by Willy Rudloff, Stuttgart, 1981.

15

Local deposits of kaolin, a fine white clay, furnish the raw materials for making pottery and porcelain at this factory in Negombo.

Independent Picture Service

Natural Resources

Precious stones are the most renowned of Sri Lanka's mineral resources. Over 90 percent of the island's gems come from a relatively small area near the southwestern city of Ratnapura, whose name means "city of gems." Gems appear amid gravel at the base of the central highlands where mountain streams have left deposits. Sri Lanka's gems include rubies, sapphires, moonstones, garnets, amethysts, topazes, cat's-eyes, tourmalines, aquamarines, and alexandrites.

Sri Lanka has become one of the world's leading producers of graphite, a material with many industrial uses. Other minerals found in Sri Lanka are mica (a thin, transparent metal), iron ore, and kaolin (a fine, white clay from which porcelain is made).

Cities

Only one-quarter of Sri Lanka's population lives in the country's urban areas, which

Photo by Bernice K. Condit

A tall statue of Gautama Buddha stands in Colombo, the capital of Sri Lanka.

16

Courtesy of Ghazali Raheem

Early colonizers erected a fort at Galle, a port city near the southern tip of the island. The city was controlled successively by Portuguese, Dutch, and British forces.

are scattered between rural communities. Nevertheless, almost every major settlement in the country is connected to the others by road or rail.

COLOMBO

The commercial capital city of Colombo has a metropolitan population of over one million people and was also the capital of the Portuguese, Dutch, and British colonial administrations in Sri Lanka. In recent times, much of Sri Lanka's governmental activity has been moved just outside the city to Sri Jayawardenepura-Kotte.

Colombo has a fine blend of architectural styles. Most of the buildings remain from British colonial times, when streets were widened and parks were created. Colorful markets, such as the Pettah, offer a wide variety of goods and stand near temples and mosques (Islamic places of worship).

Courtesy of Ghazali Raheem

The architectural style of some of Colombo's structures suggests the city's early colonial history. The old Parliament building—located on the Galle Face Green—now houses the offices of the president's administrative staff.

In 1878 the British dredged the bottom of the city's harbor and built protective seawalls. These improvements greatly expanded the capacity of the port to handle shipping, and Colombo's harbor is now the major trade center in Sri Lanka. The capital's international airport also connects flights and serves as a refueling station for major airlines.

SECONDARY CITIES

The seaport of Jaffna, at the northern peninsular tip of Sri Lanka, has a population of 271,000. Although it is located in the driest part of Sri Lanka, Jaffna has an active trade in the tobacco, cotton, timber, and fruit industries. It is also a stronghold of Tamil nationalism.

The age-old port of Galle (population 169,000) on the southern coast was known to ancient Phoenician, Greek, and Roman traders. Its geographic location on the sea route between the markets of the Middle East and south central Asia made Galle an important port until the nineteenth century, when the British developed Colombo as their main trading center.

In the central highlands of Sri Lanka lies the city of Kandy (148,000). Once the capital of a powerful Sinhalese kingdom, the city has developed into the spiritual and cultural center of the nation. In Kandy, for example, Buddhists hold an important annual religious procession, or *perahera*, and Buddhist temples and historic sites abound.

The more rugged northeastern coast contains Trincomalee (population 50,000), which is considered one of the best natural harbors in the world. The port's location was very important to the British during their rule of India and during World War II. The city handles export trade in rice, timber, and coconuts and has fine examples of religious temples and colonial architecture.

Courtesy of Ceylon Tourist Board, Colombo

Kandy's perahera actually includes five processions that occur at the same time. The most colorful of the parades leaves from the Dalada Maligawa, or Temple of the Tooth, where Sri Lanka's holiest Buddhist relic—a tooth of Gautama Buddha—is housed. Dancers and drummers surround a splendidly arrayed elephant that carries a replica of the tooth's sacred container. Among Asia's most famous ceremonies, the Kandy perahera has been celebrated for many centuries.

Elephants stand shoulder to shoulder at the Ruvanvelisaya Dagoba – a Buddhist religious monument in Anuradhapura. The Sri Lankan king Duthagamani, who ruled from 107 to 77 B.C., began the dagoba, but it was completed by his successors.

2) History and Government

Sri Lanka's earliest settlers left few records of their time on the island. In the sixth-century A.D. Buddhist monks wrote down what they knew about Sri Lanka in a chronicle called the *Mahavamsa*. The document records religious and ancient historical events and was compiled in Pali, a language that has its roots in Sanskrit— the classical language of India.

Early Period

According to the *Mahavamsa*, the Sinhalese arrived in present-day Sri Lanka from mainland India in about 500 B.C. At the head of the landing party was Vijaya, an exiled Indian prince who established a kingdom by conquering the inhabitants of the island, from whom the present-day Vedda people descend.

The newcomers, originally a northern Indian people, spoke an Indo-European language related closely to Sanskrit and more distantly to most of the languages of Europe, including English. (The modern Sinhalese language is a direct descendant of this ancient speech.)

Vijaya encouraged people from mainland India to settle on the island, and he called his realm Sinhala, after his family name. His successors ruled a region located to the north of the central highlands. Among its other achievements, the Sinhala dynasty (family of rulers) engineered an elaborate irrigation system and constructed reservoirs to store water for crops.

The Arrival of Buddhism and the Tamil

In the third century B.C., during the reign of the Sinhalese king Devanampiya Tissa, the son of the Indian emperor Asoka traveled to Sri Lanka and introduced Buddhism to the island. (Buddhism honors the ideas of the Indian philosopher Gautama Buddha.) After Devanampiya Tissa adopted Buddhism, the religion became an inseparable element of Sinhalese culture and inspired a rich and enduring artistic tradi-

Courtesy of Ghazali Raheem

An ancient sluice, or artificial passageway, regulated the Maduru Oya River, allowing its waters to flow only when they were needed.

Independent Picture Service

Scattered throughout Sri Lanka are large artificial lakes, which early kings of Sri Lanka's Sinhala dynasty erected to store water for crops.

Indian missionaries brought Buddhism to the island in the third century B.C. Eventually, much Sinhalese art depicted Gautama Buddha, an Indian prince who rejected his wealthy lifestyle to lead a more austere existence. His teachings became the basis of the Buddhist religion.

Many of the public works projects that developed under Sinhalese kings depended on a vast supply of manual laborers, who were made available to the royal government through local landowners.

tion. The new faith unified the Sinhalese under their king, and, as Buddhism disappeared in India, the Sinhalese saw themselves as the protectors of the Buddhist faith.

At roughly the same time, new arrivals —known as the Tamil—came from southern India to Sri Lanka. The Tamil spoke a Dravidian language, which was unlike any other in the region. They followed the Hindu religion, a faith with several important gods that conflicted with the strict Buddhism of the Sinhalese.

When groups of the Tamil began to settle in the northern part of Sri Lanka, the Sinhalese kings tried to stop them from establishing a community on the island. Battles between the two groups—who had sharp cultural and ethnic differences— continued for centuries. Nevertheless, the Tamil succeeded in settling northern Sri Lanka.

The Sinhala Dynasty

The country prospered under more than 90 successive kings of the Sinhala dynasty.

From the fifth century B.C. to the eleventh century A.D., art and science flourished, and a splendid capital city was laid out at Anuradhapura in the north central part of the island. The city remained the seat of government until A.D. 1017.

King Devanampiya Tissa built the first stupa—a memorial to Buddha in the form of a dome-topped mound—at Anuradhapura. Graceful rock carvings, called dagobas, stand next to the ruins of palaces, temples, and monasteries—all of which show the skill of early Sinhalese engineers. A vast network of reservoirs brought water into the city, a sewer system removed waste, and stone swimming pools provided leisure relaxation.

Sinhalese kings held complete power but, as Buddhists, had to obey strict rules regarding justice and equal treatment of their subjects. Buddhist monasteries flourished and produced fine literary and historical works, including the *Mahavamsa*. In addition, monastic elders, who organized into councils called sanghas, advised Sinhalese kings on matters of national importance.

Noble-born Sinhalese owned most of the farmland, and workers were attached by law to the land they farmed and owed loyalty and obedience to the landowner. The king's access to this free labor force was an important element in the progress of royal public works.

The vast irrigation system of tanks, canals, and sluices (water passageways) became the lifeline of the kingdom. Without it, entire agricultural estates would return to their original dry condition. As a result, Sinhalese kings worked hard to maintain peace within the realm, for conflict could easily ruin the kingdom's delicate water supply lines.

Trade with Other Lands

Because of the island's location and fertile soil, the Sinhalese kingdom attracted many visitors. In the first century A.D. the

The Ambasthale Dagoba *(far right)* at Mihintale near Anuradhapura marks the place where King Devanampiya Tissa met Mahendra, the Buddhist son of the Indian emperor Asoka. Mahendra converted the king to Buddhism, and the new religion served to unite the realm.

This fifth-century stone carving once decorated the exterior of the Isurumuniya temple near the city of Anuradhapura.

Buddhist temple entrances were often ornamented with moonstones – carved doorsteps – such as this example from the fourth century A.D.

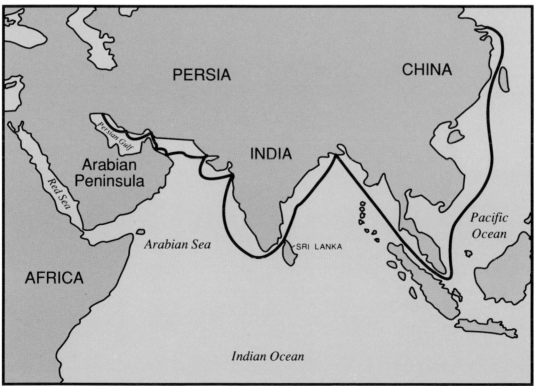

Arab traders gained control of markets in Sri Lanka – as well as in other parts of Asia – in the seventh century, when they arrived on the northwestern coast of the island.

Roman historian and geographer Pliny described the arrival in Rome of trade ambassadors from the Sinhalese kingdom. Not long after this early contact, direct trade between Sri Lanka and the Roman world began.

When the power of Rome declined in the fifth century A.D., the exchange of the island's goods with Europe became indirect, falling largely into the hands of middlepeople from the Arabian Peninsula. Arab traders—who called the island Serendib, an Arabic version of the Indian name Sinhala Dvipa—gained control of the Western trade routes to Asia in the seventh century.

In A.D. 411 the Chinese explorer Fa-hsien arrived and wrote a detailed account of his visit. As a result, commercial relations developed between Sri Lanka and China. Direct trade with China ended after Malays took over the sea-lanes to Asia in the ninth century. Nevertheless, Sinhalese ports continued to be major trading depots, and by the tenth century Galle was among the busiest ports in Asia.

The Rise of Polonnaruwa

Under the Sinhalese kingdom, the island was divided into three principal territories —Rajarata (of which Anuradhapura was the capital), Ruhuna, and Malaya. Tamil kingdoms existed in India, as well as on Sri Lanka. Sinhalese kings used the rivalry among the Indian Tamil to maintain their own security by allying with one Indian Tamil kingdom to avoid being attacked by another.

In turn, the Tamil kingdoms in southern India hoped to expand their holdings by conquering the island. One such expansionist policy was put together by the Colas, a Tamil people of southern India.

In 1017 the Colas captured the Sinhalese king Mahinda V and took him to India, where he died in 1029. Cola invaders destroyed Anuradhapura and ruled from

When the Cola dynasty took over the Sinhalese kingdom in the eleventh century, they brought their Hindu faith with them from southern India. A Hindu temple lies among the ruins of the city of Polonnaruwa, the Cola capital.

Polonnaruwa, which the newcomers established as their capital. The new north central location allowed the Colas to control overland routes to the southern territory of Ruhuna. Also during this period, Buddhism took a secondary position to the Hindu religion of the Tamil conquerors.

Resistance to Cola domination centered on Ruhuna, and in 1070 Vijayabahu I, a Sinhalese prince, overthrew the Colas and regained control of Anuradhapura. He retained Polonnaruwa as the kingdom's capital, thereby securing Sinhalese predominance in the southern and central regions of the country.

The Reign of Parakramabahu I and Its Aftermath

Civil wars followed Vijayabahu's reign, when rivals to the throne competed with one another for supremacy. Eventually, Parakramabahu I took control of Polonnaruwa, unifying Sri Lanka under his rule from 1153 to 1186. Parakramabahu reorganized the government, raised the standard of living of the people, and carried out extensive public works. He built many tanks and canals, including the massive Parakrama Samudra (Sea of Parakrama), as well as several religious monuments.

Under Parakramabahu's influence, the Sinhalese kingdom became a major power in southern Asia. Sinhalese troops invaded Burma to the northeast in about 1165, and they attacked the southern Indian kingdom of Pandya a few years later. In addition, the Sinhalese continued to launch campaigns against the Colas.

This display of energy, however, also had some negative effects. Sinhalese invasions into foreign territory brought few lasting benefits, and the extensive building schemes relied upon enormous amounts of peasant labor and government revenue. Moreover, the dynamic personality of the king—rather than a strong political and economic base—became central to the success of the realm.

Courtesy of Patrick Mendis

This statue at Polonnaruwa is believed to represent Parakramabahu I, the twelfth-century Sinhalese king who built many large structures in the city after it was recaptured by the islanders from Cola control.

When Parakramabahu died in 1186, the Sinhalese kingdom declined almost immediately. Would-be successors fought one another for control, while foreign invaders chased the royal leaders and their people farther and farther south.

A Malay invasion in the thirteenth century caused Polonnaruwa—and its extensive irrigation works—to be abandoned. With the means of agricultural prosperity disrupted, the Sinhalese kingdom divided into small realms, each with its own main city. This move encouraged other groups, such as the Tamil, to exert their power.

By the fourteenth century, southern Indian rulers had set up a Tamil kingdom on the northern Jaffna Peninsula. In the fifteenth century Chinese forces controlled the island, and Sinhalese kings paid money and handed over goods to agents of the

After the Malays and the Tamil invaded Sri Lanka in the thirteenth and fourteenth centuries, Polonnaruwa was abandoned. Its extensive buildings—such as the royal palace—fell into ruin.

Courtesy of Ghazali Raheem

Chinese Empire. When Europeans arrived in the early sixteenth century, a Sinhalese leader ruled from Kotte near present-day Colombo, and another held power in Kandy, a city in the central highlands.

The Arrival of the Portuguese

In the late fifteenth century the search for new markets reopened trade routes between Europe and India. As a result, Portuguese navigators visited Sri Lanka in 1505, docking near Colombo to find cinnamon and other spices. Within a few years the Portuguese were in virtual control of most of the coastal regions of the island, although they did not assume formal rule until 1597.

The Portuguese primarily wanted to control production of the island's spices. As a result, they attempted to conquer the Sri Lankan interior—where spice plants grew in abundance. Resistance to the Portuguese came from the mountain kingdom of Kandy. The Kandyans withstood Portuguese efforts to absorb them, and the Portuguese settled for acquiring only coastal areas of Sri Lanka, which they collectively called Ceilao (a variation of the Arabic name Serendib).

Portugal's period of control brought several major changes to the island. The Portuguese introduced Christianity in the form of Roman Catholicism, brought in Western styles of education, and developed the port of Colombo into a major trading center.

The Portuguese cemented anticolonial feeling among the Sinhalese by following a policy of intolerance toward other religions. They destroyed Hindu and Buddhist temples and persecuted Muslim traders who lived along the coast. Resistance to Portuguese rule centered on Kandy, the still-independent Sinhalese kingdom in the central highlands.

The Dutch Takeover

In 1638 the Netherlands—a rival European trading power—drove the Portuguese out by making an alliance with the Kandyan kingdom. In exchange for a share of the cinnamon lands located in Kandy, the Dutch agreed to take the island's port cities from the Portuguese and to return them to the Sinhalese. In this way, the Sinhalese recaptured Trincomalee and Batticaloa, but the Dutch retained the ports of Galle and Negombo and began to collect revenue from them. In time, the Dutch also tried to subdue Kandy but, like the Portuguese, failed.

Unable to control all of the profitable cinnamon lands, the Dutch began to cultivate the spice in the lowlands. They also grew plantation crops, including coffee, coconuts, sugarcane, cotton, and tobacco. The most important Dutch legacy, however, was the introduction of Roman-Dutch laws, which covered property and inheritance rights.

British Influence

In the seventeenth and eighteenth centuries, another strong European power—Great Britain—also became active in the Indian Ocean. Through the British East

Courtesy of Ghazali Raheem

Europeans established the first plantations, which grew crops—such as coffee, sugarcane, tobacco, and tea—for export.

India Company—a trading agency chartered by the British government—Britain gained control over the Indian subcontinent. In addition, Britain wanted a militarily safe, all-weather port to protect its holdings in eastern India. The Dutch agreed to allow the British to use Trincomalee as a naval base.

Friendly relations between the Dutch and the British deteriorated in the late eighteenth century, and the Dutch withdrew permission to use Trincomalee. The British captured the port in 1796, effectively ending Dutch power on the island. Thereafter, Britain—first through its delegates in India and later directly—administered the island.

Initially, the British held only the coastal areas, as the two previous European powers had; the Kandyan kingdom remained independent. To consolidate their island holdings, the British declared their lands in Sri Lanka—which they called Ceylon, after the Portuguese Ceilao, to be a colony in 1802. Meanwhile, internal dissension in Kandy weakened the kingdom, making way for British campaigns against the highland realm.

The Nineteenth Century

Conflicts between the Sinhalese king Sri Wickrama Rajasinghe and his nobles helped the British to take over Kandy. Kandyan rebels invited the British to intervene in the dispute, and the royal Kandyan troops laid down their weapons without actually fighting Britain's forces. The British captured the king and sent him to southern India in 1815, after which the British and Sinhalese signed a treaty that formally ended hostilities.

Anticolonial rebellions flared in the next three years, however, among both Buddhist clergy and Sinhalese nobles, who felt edged out of power. In 1818 the British stopped using local Sri Lankan administrations to govern and later divided Kandy among surrounding provinces.

Large-scale agricultural development emerged in Ceylon during the nineteenth century. At first, the British raised coffee

Independent Picture Service   Independent Picture Service

The British encouraged workers from nearby India to emigrate to the colony they named Ceylon (modern Sri Lanka). Laborers harvested latex (a milky substance) from rubber trees (left) **and plucked the leaves from tea plants** (right).

During the nineteenth century, the British established colonial regiments, whose officers were British. Here, members of the Ceylon mounted infantry gather on the island in 1897.

on their major estates, but low market prices and disease caused the British to replace this product with tea. Rubber and coconuts also found a steady market value and became important export crops. The plantation system required a large labor force—larger than the island's population could provide. As a result, the British began to encourage Tamil emigration from southern India.

In addition to developing an export economy, the British established road and rail connections to aid plantation owners. The British educational system—another important colonial innovation—began to Westernize new generations of Sinhalese and Tamil, mostly for posts in the Ceylon Civil Service. Because they saw advantages in cooperating with the British, the Tamil held numerous posts at all levels of the colonial administration.

Reform Movements

After more than 75 years of British rule, reform movements among local peoples—

especially Buddhist monks and Ceylonese professionals—began to emerge. The Jaffna Association, the Ceylon National Association, and other groups agitated for changes in policy that would allow them more political power. In addition, a Buddhist movement encouraged people to return Buddhism to its dominant role in island society. Although they conflicted, both monks and professionals ultimately desired independence. The professionals wanted to gain a more active role in the colonial government. The Buddhists sought to eliminate Western influence and to strengthen Buddhism's status in the country.

The British tried to ease the conflicts by making minor policy changes, but the effort failed to calm the activists' concerns. Nationalists organized a railway strike in 1912, and the event stirred anticolonial sentiments among the colony's writers and poets. In 1915, after a religious disturbance occurred between Buddhists and Muslims, the British declared martial law (rule by the military) on the island. Harsh

Courtesy of Ceylon Tourist Board, Colombo

Buddhist monks — who traditionally wear orange robes — played an important role in the island's government under Sinhalese kings. Groups of monks formed advisory councils, called sanghas, but under British rule they had less influence over political and social affairs.

Independent Picture Service

Swami Rock at Trincomalee lies just beyond Fort Frederick, a stronghold originally built by the Portuguese that continues to be used as a military outpost.

measures, including arbitrary arrests and killings, formed nationalist feelings into a driving force. As a consequence, the Ceylon National Congress, whose aim was to secure self-government for Ceylon, was established in 1919.

From Britain's point of view, the question was how to retain control of Ceylon's commerce, industry, and ports while giving the Ceylonese limited self-government. The British decided to write a constitution that would include more representation for local peoples. British control would remain in force through the document's newly formed States Council.

The Road to Independence

Agitations for Ceylonese independence continued when World War II broke out in Southeast Asia in 1941. The British lost their port at Singapore to the Japanese, and, as a result, Trincomalee regained its position as a strategic outpost. The British recognized that a loyal colonial population would help them to win the war in the region. They promised self-government to the Ceylonese after global hostilities were over in order to gain the cooperation of the islanders during the war.

In 1946 the postwar British government in London approved the first Ceylonese constitution. The document had come about largely through the efforts of D. S. Senanayake, the colonial administration's minister of agriculture. In 1947, following widespread strikes, the British granted Ceylon commonwealth status, meaning that the former colony was self-governing but still associated with Great Britain. A majority of voters supported Senanayake's United National party (UNP) —a coalition of the Ceylon National Congress, the Sinhala Maha Sabha party, and the Muslim League. On February 4, 1948, Ceylon became a fully independent nation with Senanayake as its first prime minister.

Early Administrations

The UNP held power from 1948 to 1956. D. S. Senanayake encouraged private enterprise and organized programs to raise the standard of living for Ceylonese citizens. Irrigation and hydroelectrical power plants brought needed agricultural improvements to the dry zone. The government built more schools, provided free education, and brought dangerous diseases, such as malaria, under control.

D. S. Senanayake died in a horse-riding accident in 1952, and his death destabilized the UNP. Senanayake's son Dudley, who had been educated in Britain, led the government until riots in 1953 forced him to resign. His cousin, the equally Westernized Sir John Kotelawala, followed him in office.

The civil flag of the Dominion of Ceylon was adopted at independence in 1948 and remained in use until 1951.

Artwork by Steven Woods

Independent Picture Service

Dudley Senanayake served as prime minister of Sri Lanka (then called Ceylon) several times during the period from 1953 to 1970.

Buddhist nationalism—a force that independence had not really calmed—continued to grow, however. Conservative Buddhists wanted Ceylon to return to its Sinhalese Buddhist origins, under which the clergy had great authority within the political structure. Giving direction to this nationalist movement was a Western-educated Sinhalese—S. W. R. D. Bandaranaike, leader of the Sinhala Maha Sabha. In 1951 he left the UNP and renamed his wing of the organization the Sri Lanka Freedom party (SLFP), which won the general elections of 1956.

Bandaranaike's government introduced socialist reforms, including the nationalization (change from private to government ownership) of plantations and banks. The regime also maintained a position of nonalignment, or neutrality, toward the Soviet Union and the United States. Most important, however, was Bandaranaike's decision to establish Sinhalese as the country's official language—a move that underscored the nation's independence from its colonial past and the dominance of the Sinhalese majority.

The Tamil reacted strongly to this move, which they considered a ploy to decrease their political influence and opportunities. Eventually, Bandaranaike agreed to make Tamil a national language in the northern and eastern provinces, where the Tamil were in the majority. But the language issue fanned an ethnic conflict that has continued for decades.

The Modern Era

A Buddhist monk assassinated Prime Minister Bandaranaike in 1959, and since then political power has alternated between the UNP and the SLFP. Bandaranaike's widow Sirimavo won the 1960 elections and became the first woman in the world to serve as prime minister. She continued to pursue the ideas supported by her husband, but her government faced economic difficulties as well as ethnic clashes.

In 1965 Dudley Senanayake succeeded Sirimavo Bandaranaike, and his UNP administration imposed states of emergency, which increased ethnic tensions. Elections in 1970 returned Bandaranaike to office, but she faced a rebel youth movement, called the Janatha Vimukti Peramuna (People's Liberation Front). The move-

Independent Picture Service

Prime Minister S. W. R. D. Bandaranaike initiated nationalization programs that shifted ownership of plantations—including ones that grew sugarcane—from private to government hands.

ment's leaders, who were Communists, sought to overthrow the SLFP government, because they felt Communism would solve Ceylon's economic and cultural problems. By the time the government suppressed the youth revolt in late 1971, thousands of Ceylonese had been killed. The prime minister declared a state of emergency, which remained in effect for six years.

In 1972 the Ceylonese legislature adopted a new constitution, which renamed Ceylon the Socialist Republic of Sri Lanka. Although it eliminated the British-held post of governor-general, the constitution left Sri Lanka within the British Commonwealth.

By mid-1973 the Tamil minority in the north had begun to demand a separate, independent state. No longer highly placed throughout Sri Lanka's civil service and educational system, the Tamil felt discriminated against in public employment, in university entrance, and in land grants. The two major Tamil political parties jointly formed the Tamil United Front (TUF), which aimed to protect and promote Tamil interests and to resolve Tamil grievances. The TUF eventually changed its name to the Tamil United Liberation Front (TULF) and actively supported the idea of Tamil Eelam—the name of the proposed independent nation.

In addition to creating the Sri Lankan republic, the Constitution of 1972 introduced the office of executive president, although the prime minister still possessed great political power. In the election campaign of 1977, the UNP advocated a much stronger role for the president. Under the leadership of J. R. Jayewardene, the party won the elections and passed another constitution that reorganized the executive branch. The document gave more political power to the office of the president, who would be directly elected. The constitution also changed the name of the country to the Democratic Socialist Republic of Sri Lanka.

Independent Picture Service

Sirimavo Bandaranaike, the first woman in the world to serve as a prime minister, initially came to power in 1960. In 1980 a presidential commission withheld her civic rights for political abuses while in office. The rights were reinstated in 1986.

Independent Picture Service

The Sri Lankan unit of money is the rupee, and the government issues coins that represent one, two, and five rupees.

Independent Picture Service

Sri Lankan administrations initiated efforts in the 1960s and 1970s to increase the nation's foreign income from tourism and developed the ancient capital of Polonnaruwa, for example, into a popular attraction. Ethnic violence in the 1980s, however, has substantially affected this segment of the nation's economy.

Civil Strife Increases

In the 1980s Sri Lanka was nearly in a state of civil war. The Tamil rebellion, led by well-trained guerrillas and aimed at civilian as well as military targets, disrupted the northern third of the country. The disturbances caused conflicts even within the Sinhalese majority. Some Sinhalese wanted to negotiate an agreement, while others favored a military solution.

In 1983 the TULF—the largest opposition party in the Sri Lankan Parliament—boycotted legislative activity. The party's delegates refused to take a constitutional oath that barred any citizen from encouraging the establishment of a separate state within Sri Lanka. The UNP-dominated legislature took the TULF boycott to mean that the Tamil delegates had forfeited their seats. Tamil representation has since been absent from the Sri Lankan Parliament.

Despite President Jayewardene's attempts in 1984 and 1985 to develop a dialogue with formal Tamil political parties, Tamil guerrilla groups continued to fight. In response, Sri Lanka's army began to take revenge on civilian Tamil populations. Thousands of Tamil and Sinhalese have been killed or have been left homeless by the violence.

Tamil guerrillas in Sri Lanka have received funding, training, and refuge from the state of Tamil Nadu in southeastern India. Because Sri Lanka's Tamil have a cultural and religious connection with the Tamil of Tamil Nadu, India's prime minister Rajiv Gandhi tried to help solve the conflict on the nearby island. India's government wished not only to avoid a similar uprising within its own territory but also to retain Indian Tamil political support.

In July 1987 Gandhi signed a peace agreement with President Jayewardene,

Bettmann Newsphotos

Sri Lankan president J. R. Jayewardene *(left)* shakes hands with India's prime minister Rajiv Gandhi before an Asian summit meeting in 1986. The two leaders signed a peace agreement in 1987 that has not yet calmed ethnic tensions on the island.

A member of the Liberation Tigers of Tamil Eelam, a Tamil guerrilla force, aims a rocket grenade launcher at a target on the Jaffna Peninsula. Conflicts between Tamil, Sinhalese, and Indian forces have damaged many parts of the peninsula and have left many people homeless.

The design of Sri Lanka's flag became official in 1978, after Ceylon had changed its name to Sri Lanka. In 1951 the green and orange stripes had been added to the original flag to represent the island's Muslim and Hindu minorities, respectively. The sword-carrying lion is an ancient Kandyan image, and the four pipal leaves symbolize the sacred bo tree, under which Gautama Buddha sat while gaining enlightenment.

Violence between ethnic groups occasionally erupts in the south. Here, a Tamil-owned house in Colombo burns out of control after being set on fire by Sinhalese.

Photo by Drs. A. A. M. van der Heyden, Naarden, the Netherlands

and a 20,000-person peacekeeping force arrived from India to disarm the rebels and to quiet the violence. But the main Tamil rebel group has rejected the agreement, and Indian troops are now fighting a war outside their borders. In spite of Indian aid, India's regional domination may be the one thing that both the Sinhalese and the Tamil can agree they want to avoid.

Government

Under the Constitution of 1977, Sri Lanka changed its political framework from a British-style parliamentary model to an elected presidential system. The executive president, who is also head of state and commander of the armed forces, is elected directly by the people to a six-year term. The president is responsible to Parliament for the exercise of presidential duties and may be removed from office by a two-thirds majority vote of the legislature.

The president appoints the prime minister, who is the leader of the ruling party in the legislature and the head of the cabinet. The president also appoints other cabinet ministers, deputy ministers, and noncabinet ministers.

Parliament is a unicameral (one-house) body whose members are elected to six-year terms by Sri Lankans who are 18 years of age or older. In 1988 Parliament consisted of 168 members, but recent legislation increased the number to 196 in order to meet new rules of proportional representation. This change will make the number of delegates from each party in Parliament reflect the percentages of votes that the parties win in elections.

Courtesy of Ghazali Raheem

The Sri Lankan Parliament's new assembly rooms are in Sri Jayawardenepura-Kotte, just outside of Colombo.

36

Until it was dissolved in the 1970s, the upper house of the Sri Lankan Parliament met in this arcaded building in Colombo. Today the structure serves as the headquarters of the Ministry of Defense.

Sri Lanka's judiciary system consists of a supreme court, a court of appeals, a high court, and a number of lower courts. Parliament may create additional tribunals and may amend judiciary powers.

The legal system is a reflection of past colonial and cultural influences. For example, criminal laws follow the same framework as British laws, while civil law is of Roman-Dutch origin. Personal laws—relating to marriage, divorce, and inheritance—are unique to each ethnic group on the island. Kandyan law, for instance, applies to the central highlands, Thesavalamai law is for the northern Tamil community, and Muslims are governed by an Islamic code.

Sri Lanka is divided into 25 administrative districts. A government agent, who is a member of the Sri Lankan civil service, is responsible for all government activities in the district. Regional, city, and village councils are elected locally and have limited powers.

The government adopted a system of free education soon after independence, and since then most schools in Sri Lanka have been run by the state.

Courtesy of Nathan Rabe

3) The People

About three-quarters of Sri Lanka's nearly 17 million people live in rural areas, with about 4 million residing in the wet zone, where agricultural conditions are most favorable. Nevertheless, the suburbs and city of Colombo, whose urban facilities promise the greatest number of job opportunities, have over one million people.

Although legally discouraged, the remnants of a caste system—which separates society into rigid social and professional classes—exists in Sri Lanka, mainly in rural areas. Members of one family generally remain in the same caste, and marriages are usually arranged within a caste. Although Buddhism rejects social barriers, Sinhalese Buddhists live by caste rules. Hinduism includes a caste system, but the Sri Lankan Tamil follow an arrangement that is different from the one supported by the Tamil in India. With the spread of education, caste differences are disappearing, especially in the areas of job selection and work opportunities.

Ethnic Groups

In Sri Lankan society, many languages, ethnic groups, and religions exist side by side. The Sinhalese are the major ethnic community, making up 74 percent of the population. They are primarily Buddhists, but some are Christians. Two different Sinhalese groups—one in the highlands and the other in the low country—live in Sri Lanka.

Because of their relative isolation from European influences and developments, highland Sinhalese tend to be socially and politically conservative. They make up roughly 40 percent of the Sinhalese population. The remaining low-country Sinhalese—who have constantly been in contact with new cultures arriving on the coasts—generally have a broader outlook. Most Sinhalese of both subgroups are farmers who raise rice and other crops in villages.

The Tamil compose about 18 percent of the population and are mostly Hindus. About two-thirds are Sri Lankan Tamil whose ancestors have lived on the island (especially in northern areas of the Jaffna

A Sinhalese family walks along a beach in southern Sri Lanka. Most low-country Sinhalese live in coastal areas, where they—like highland Sinhalese—raise rice and fruits.

Peninsula) for many centuries. They are involved in trade and other business activities in major cities, and some hold prominent government jobs throughout Sri Lanka. The other third are Indian Tamil—the descendants of southern Indians who worked on the British-owned tea plantations in the nineteenth century. Most Indian Tamil still make their livelihoods in the central tea estates.

Other minority groups include Muslims, Burghers—the mixed descendants of Europeans and Sinhalese—and Malays, who together make up about 8 percent of the population. A small number of Vedda, who are believed to be descendants of the country's first known inhabitants, live in remote communities on the island.

Religion and Festivals

The form of the Buddhist religion practiced in Sri Lanka is known as Theravada

Independent Picture Service

This Anuradhapura stone carving stands at the entrance to the sacred bo tree. The tree grew from a cutting of the original bo tree that was brought to Sri Lanka by the sister of Mahendra—the Indian prince who introduced Buddhism to Sri Lanka over 2,000 years ago.

Independent Picture Service

The dry Jaffna Peninsula is home to many of Sri Lanka's Tamil. Here, members of this ethnic community draw water from a deep well.

Buddhism (Theravada means teachings of the elders), and about 70 percent of the people support it. The underlying belief of Buddhism is that human suffering arises from the selfish desire for comfort and luxury. As laid down by Gautama Buddha—who founded the religion in India in the sixth century B.C.—the way to put an end to desire is to follow eight rules of conduct.

In Buddhist thought, bhikkus—monks who reject luxury and who follow this eightfold path—are the only people who will be able to achieve the highest state of understanding, called nirvana. A group of bhikkus forms a sangha, which historically has been among the most important social and religious organizations in Sri Lanka. Bhikkus live according to the strictest interpretation of Theravada Buddhism, but ordinary people follow the Buddhist faith to a lesser degree and worship many regional gods, mainly of Hindu origin.

According to tradition, the Kelaniya Raja Maha Vihara was built on a spot where Gautama Buddha preached. The temple, which is located near Colombo, is the focus of a major Buddhist perahera held annually in January.

The strong sense of Buddhist family unity is clearly displayed during the festivals associated with New Year's Day, which occurs in mid-April. Buddhists wear new clothes, beat traditional brass drums (*rabanas*), set off fireworks, and eat special delicacies. Believers look for good omens when they light the first hearth fire and when they eat the first meal of the new year.

In late July or in August, depending on when the full moon falls, several of the nation's many peraheras (Buddhist processions) are held. The most important perahera, which takes place in Kandy, is a formal parade for a sacred memento of Gautama Buddha. Heavily festooned elephants, flashy drums, traditional dancers, and colorful flowers are seen during this sacred Buddhist holiday.

Photo by Ruthi Soudack

Dozens of decorated elephants and hundreds of dancers participate in the 10-day celebration of the Kandy perahera.

Photo by Christopher Cormack

Statues of Gautama Buddha often depict him wearing the orange robes now worn by Buddhist monks and sitting with his legs crossed in the lotus position used in meditation.

Called *kovils* in Sri Lanka, Hindu temples—such as this one near Puttalam on the western coast of the island—often feature a multitude of small, colorful carvings and are dedicated to one of Hinduism's several gods.

Two Buddhist monks share an umbrella against the sun at Anuradhapura.

Most Tamil practice Hinduism and worship several gods, the most important of which are Brahma, Siva, and Vishnu. They also accept the four Vedas (collections of sacred hymns) as Hindu religious writings, worship cows as symbols of holiness and purity, and have a caste system. Much of daily Hindu worship in Sri Lanka takes place within the home, although temples are the focus for the more important annual rituals, such as New Year and Dewali (Festival of Lights).

About 8 percent of the population—both Sinhalese and Tamil—are Christians, mainly Roman Catholics. The Christian faith has existed in Sri Lanka since the arrival of the Portuguese, who converted many coastal peoples. Protestantism arrived with the Dutch and the British, but

A mosque (Islamic place of prayer) stands inside the fort at Galle in southern Sri Lanka.

missionary efforts failed to develop a large Protestant community on the island.

The Islamic religion, founded in Arabia in the seventh century A.D., arrived in Sri Lanka via Arab traders. Supporters of the faith—called Muslims—come from Sri Lanka's Malay and Arab populations. Approximately 8 percent of Sri Lanka's population, mostly in the coastal regions, follow Islam.

Health

Although health conditions in Sri Lanka are the best in southern Asia, differences exist between urban and rural areas. A higher standard of living in the cities, where the availability of frequent medical care is greater, is evident in low infant mortality rates and long life expectancy. Nationwide, life expectancy in Sri Lanka is 70 years, and the infant mortality rate is 30 deaths per 1,000 live births. Both figures compare favorably with other nations in the region.

In a forest clearing, villagers use a newly installed well that has helped to reduce diseases related to impure water.

Only about one-fourth of Sri Lanka's population have access to safe drinking water. Many wells are unprotected from fouling by animals and are poorly maintained.

Courtesy of UNICEF

Widespread campaigns, aimed at curing tuberculosis, malaria, and childhood diseases, have bettered health conditions throughout the nation. Nevertheless, ailments spread by impure food and water are still common. Rapid population growth has made it difficult for the nation's health department to keep pace with the need for new sewage and water systems. Only about 26 percent of the rural population have access to safe drinking water, although it is available to about 76 percent of urban dwellers.

In addition to doctors and other modern medical personnel, some Sri Lankans who live in rural areas go to practitioners of Ayurveda for their health needs. Ayurvedic physicians use traditional herbal medicines to treat the sick, and registered Ayurvedics are recognized by the government's Ministry of Health.

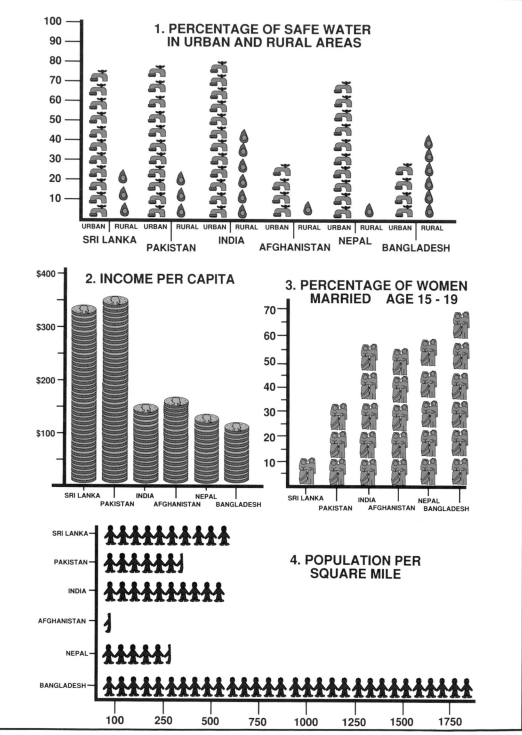

1. PERCENTAGE OF SAFE WATER IN URBAN AND RURAL AREAS

2. INCOME PER CAPITA

3. PERCENTAGE OF WOMEN MARRIED   AGE 15 - 19

4. POPULATION PER SQUARE MILE

Artwork by Mindy A. Rabin

Depicted in this chart are factors relating to the standard of living in six countries in southern Asia. Information taken from "1987 World Population Data Sheet," "The World's Women: A Profile," and "Children of the World" compiled by the Population Reference Bureau, Washington, D.C.

Sri Lankans have made great strides in education, with the result that 91 percent of males and 83 percent of females can read and write.

Education

Before the Europeans came, Buddhist monks were responsible for most educational training. Later, the Portuguese established Roman Catholic schools, and the Dutch organized Protestant institutions. Although the British founded many Protestant missions, the colonial government also provided financial support to schools of the Buddhist and Hindu faiths. The instructors taught in English, however, at the expense of the student's knowledge of local languages and cultures.

After independence, the government developed a system of free education from kindergarten through the university level, with Sinhalese as the first language and English as a compulsory second language. Tamil children were educated in Tamil from primary through university classes. In 1987 almost 90 percent of the population could read and write.

School attendance is compulsory for children from the ages of 6 to 14, and about 85 percent of the school-aged population are enrolled in classes. Both private and state-run schools exist, although state-run schools are more numerous. Private schools, such as the Buddhist *pirivenas,* include their own subjects—Buddhist studies, for example—but must comply with national laws regarding educational content in order to receive state funds. The main institution of higher learning was the University of Ceylon until the 1980s, when its secondary campuses became independent universities.

Language and Literature

In 1956 the government made Sinhalese the official language of Sri Lanka, and now more than 70 percent of the population speak it. After strong demonstrations by the Tamil minority, Tamil was made a national language in 1978 and is used in all administrative affairs of the northern and eastern provinces. English—the official language under British rule—is still spoken throughout the country.

Sinhalese uses written symbols derived from the Brahmi script of ancient Indian languages. One letter does not necessarily represent a single sound but instead may stand for a consonant and a vowel together. Tamil has its own script, which is also derived from Brahmi but which is quite distinct from Sinhalese.

The literature of Sri Lanka goes back to the third century B.C., when Mahendra, an Indian prince, introduced Buddhism to the island. The written tradition includes ancient chronicles—such as the *Mahavamsa* —which preserve religious and historical events. Pali—the northern Indian language used to record Buddhist teachings and traditions—continues to be the classical language of Theravada Buddhism in Sri Lanka. Most early Sinhalese literature is based on translations of works originally composed in Pali.

In time, the Sinhalese developed their own literature. Among the best-known literary classics are the thirteenth-century *Kavsilumina*, a long romantic poem, and collections of writings, called Jatakas, concerning the life of Buddha.

The modern era produced Sinhalese novelists, such as Piyadasa Sirisena, who brought nationalist themes to their work. Others, like W. A. Silva, were famous for their ability to tell a good story, often based on historical events. In the late twentieth century, novelists have attempted to deal with current issues, such as modernization versus tradition in Sri Lankan society.

Architecture and the Arts

Ancient Sinhalese sculpture and architecture stretch over a 1,500-year period. The cities of Anuradhapura and Polonnaruwa have some of the world's greatest architectural treasures. Highly skilled artisans carved gigantic statues, dagobas, and the entrances to palaces and temples. Massive shrines contrast with delicate art forms, like those used to make the pillars of

Much of Sri Lanka's early literature focused on the life of Gautama Buddha, sculpted here in a reclining position at Polonnaruwa.

Independent Picture Service

The Thuparama Dagoba is the oldest bell-shaped shrine at Anuradhapura and was constructed during the reign of King Devanampiya Tissa in the third century B.C.

Nissanka Latha Mandapaya, which are carved in the shape of lotus blossoms.

The oldest remaining examples of early painting—and the only ones that do not deal with religious subjects—are at Sigiriya, west of Polonnaruwa. The frescoes (paintings on plaster) portray large-eyed women with faint smiles in subtle shades of red, yellow, and green.

Modern schools of painting and sculpture have experimented with impressionist and abstract styles that use both Western and local themes. Artists, such as Senaka Senanayake and Tissa Ranasinghe, have exhibited internationally and receive commissions from Sri Lankan businesses, Buddhist temples, and occasionally the government.

Courtesy of Ghazali Raheem

Playful sculpted images decorate the Kelaniya temple near Colombo.

A long, sheltered rock gallery at Sigiriya – an ancient fortress in central Sri Lanka – provided the surface for 22 paintings of Sinhalese women that date from the fifth century A.D.

The Sri Lankan government encourages the production of local crafts, such as painted textiles (right) and wood carvings (below).

Cottage industries, in which craft products are made in the home or in village workshops, are an important aspect of Sri Lankan life. Most Sinhalese craftspeople live in small villages, and their output is of considerable value to the economy of the country.

Toys, walking sticks, and ashtrays covered with a shiny varnish, called lacquer, are famous throughout Sri Lanka, and artisans produce delicate handmade lace in Galle. Kalutara, south of Colombo, is renowned for its baskets, sandals, sun hats, table mats, and other woven objects. The Sri Lankan government encourages local enterprises through its support of training schools and through its assistance in finding markets and raw materials for craftspeople.

Food, Clothing, and Housing

Rice is the basis of the daily Sri Lankan diet. A heaping dish of rice and curry (a food that is seasoned with a blend of strong spices of the same name) is the customary main meal of the day for rural residents. It is served in the evening, usually with fruit as a second course. Tea is served with most meals and as a refreshment. Most Buddhists obey the religious ban against eating meat, but they often consume fish with rice and curry. A great variety of seasonings adds diversity to the curries, and a wide range of fruits—such as bananas, coconuts, mangoes, papayas, oranges, pineapples, and pomegranates —supplement plain rice.

Sri Lankan cuisine has absorbed elements from its many influential cultures. As a result, Dutch Christmas cake, called *broeder*, and Portuguese cookies, known as *boroa*, have found their way into Sri Lanka's cooking. Tamil traditions include *thosai* (pancakes) and *vade* (spicy doughnuts), and Muslims make *wattalapam*— coconut milk pudding.

A market stall displays some of the foods available in Sri Lanka, including fish, fruit, and spices.

Photo by Drs. A. A. M. van der Heyden, Naarden, the Netherlands

Courtesy of UNICEF

A family prays before eating a meal of rice and fruit.

51

Wearing a *camboy,* or sarong and blouse, a nursery-school teacher observes the painting technique of one of her young students.

A streetside pineapple vendor is dressed in a sarong—a long wrap-around garment—and a shirt.

Although Western-style clothing is often seen in urban areas, villagers continue to dress traditionally. For men, this means a sarong (a wrap-around garment that forms a long skirt) and a collarless shirt. Most Sri Lankan women wear saris (large pieces of cloth that are draped around the body like long dresses) or *camboys,* which consist of a sarong and a blouse.

Most Sri Lankans live in rural areas, generally in villages made up of small dwellings. One-story urban houses are often crowded together, with a garden at the back. To increase the number of rural and urban houses and to improve their quality, Sri Lanka's government has sponsored the Million Houses Program, which aims to build a million new homes by the year 2000. The plan involves substantial local participation in order to gather resources and to promote community decision making.

Most of Sri Lanka's inhabitants live in small thatched dwellings *(right).* The shortage and poor quality of homes in Sri Lanka encouraged the government to launch the Million Houses Program, which has resulted in new housing in a suburb of Colombo *(below).*

Courtesy of Cheryl Pattison

Courtesy of Cheryl Pattison

Workers walk along raised barriers between rice paddies. Despite increases in crop volumes, the government still imports large quantities of rice.

4) The Economy

When the Europeans first established large plantations at the beginning of the nineteenth century, much of the land that had formerly produced foods for local consumption was devoted to growing crops for export. Sri Lanka achieved international fame for its spices during the early colonial period and later for its coffee, tea, coconuts, and rubber. Although this level of diversity generated a large income for the country, it did not feed Sri Lanka's growing population.

Postindependence governments have tried to increase local food production without reducing the crops that earn money abroad. But Sri Lanka still spends more money on food imports than it earns from the export of its chief crops. In addition, the Sri Lankan government wants to develop industry—in the making of textiles, fertilizers, cement, iron, steel, and rubber products—in order to broaden its predominantly agricultural economy.

Agriculture

The agricultural sector employs about one-half of the work force and provides about one-third of the nation's income. Roughly five million acres are under cultivation, approximately 62 percent of which lie in the southwestern wet zone. Sri Lanka ranks second after India in world tea production, third after Malaysia and Indonesia in the output of rubber, and is a world leader in coconut yields.

About two-thirds of the nation's farmland needs to be irrigated, and the government has restored some of the old irrigation systems to provide more water. In addition, the Mahaweli River development project will water new areas.

DOMESTIC PRODUCTION

Rice, grown on about 1.5 million acres of land, is Sri Lanka's main food crop and, in volume, is the largest single domestic crop grown in the country. In the mid-1980s Sri Lanka harvested over 2.5 million tons of rice each year, but large quantities of the grain still had to be imported.

Secondary crops include cassavas, coffee, tobacco, and cacao (from which chocolate is made), as well as spices such as cardamom, cinnamon, and pepper. In the nineteenth century planters grew coffee extensively, but within a few decades the product lost ground to tea. In the 1980s the government encouraged coffee production in the hope of bringing back the income once gained from the commodity.

Sri Lankan farmers raise more than 1.7 million cattle, 910,000 buffalo, 520,000 goats, and 77,000 pigs. Herders raise cattle mainly for their milk and as work animals. Since farming is done largely without the aid of modern machinery, animals perform important agricultural tasks, and buffalo, as well as oxen, are used to pull the plows.

As part of a project to improve livestock, the government is crossbreeding zebus—noted for their ability to endure heat and to resist disease—with milk-rich Jersey cattle from Great Britain. The government hopes that a stronger, more productive breed of cow will result.

Courtesy of World Bank

Sri Lankan laborers plant rice seedlings by hand in an irrigated field.

Photo by Ruthi Soudack

After a rice crop is harvested, an ox-pulled plow turns the earth for replanting.

The tea plants of a large estate in the central highlands cover the hills as well as the level ground.

Cables carry sacks of freshly picked tea to factories for further processing.

Courtesy of Nathan Rabe

Tea pickers appear as small white specks on a tea-covered mountainside near Kandy.

Independent Picture Service

At the factory, tea leaves are spread on racks where they are left to dry for about 18 hours.

Coconuts come from trees on small holdings that are located primarily along the southwestern coast. The unripe fruit contains a refreshing drink, the coarse fibers (called coir) of the husk can be woven into bags or mats, and the coconut's meat may be shredded as a food. Unlike tea and rubber, coconuts have a large market within Sri Lanka, as well as abroad.

EXPORT CROPS

Still marketed as Ceylon tea because of its international reputation by that name, Sri Lankan tea grows at many elevations. Plants at the highest altitudes are the choicest and bear the classification high-grown if they come from slopes over 4,000 feet above sea level. Medium-grown tea is from bushes planted between 2,000 and 4,000 feet high, and any tea from lower altitudes is called low-grown. The government owns most of the tea estates, although small landowners contribute substantially to the industry's total output.

Rubber plantations are located in low, hot areas of the southwest, where the amount of rainfall is more than 80 inches annually. Like tea estates, the large rubber plantations have been taken over by the government and, combined with the many small acreages that are privately owned, account for Sri Lanka's rubber production.

Courtesy of Nathan Rabe

A worker husks a pile of coconuts, a process that strips the fibrous shell—used to make twine—from the inner flesh of the nut.

At Ja-ela, north of Colombo, small ponds have been built among coconut groves to promote the island's fishing industry.

Courtesy of Patrick Mendis

Photo by Ruthi Soudack

Fishermen pull their ocean catch ashore at Uppuveli, near Trincomalee.

Forestry and Fisheries

The forests of Sri Lanka were once far more extensive than they are now. Many acres of valuable native trees, such as the calamander, have been cleared to expand farming plots and pastureland. To offset the destruction of this natural resource, the government sponsors reforestation schemes and plants teak, eucalyptus, mahogany, and other commercially profitable trees. Sri Lankans use most of the harvested wood for domestic fuel and for building materials, although some tree plantations supply the pulp industry.

Two kinds of fishing industries exist in Sri Lanka. A small inland industry based on reservoirs contributes to the daily diet of rural people. Ocean fishing in coastal areas that are not part of the nation's network of wildlife preserves is done on a

Modernization of Sri Lanka's textile mills has increased the production of cloth—a major manufacturing item on the island.

larger scale. Nevertheless, the total fishing industry brings relatively little to the national economy, and annual fishing hauls in the 1980s amounted to only about 170,000 tons.

Mining and Industry

Sri Lanka has limited mineral resources, except for large deposits of high-grade graphite. Companies mine ilmenite (a black ore), rutile (a reddish-black mineral), and zircon (a hard, brown substance) for commercial use. Limestone is extracted for a government-owned cement corporation at Kankesanthurai on the Jaffna Peninsula. Other minerals include salt, mica, and sands that are employed in glassmaking.

The valleys around the city of Ratnapura contain a wide variety of precious and semiprecious stones, including sapphires, rubies, aquamarines, moonstones, and topazes. Sri Lanka also has deposits of kaolin, which is used by ceramic companies.

Sri Lankans in search of precious stones sift muddy water through straw strainers not far from the city of Ratnapura.

At Elephant Pass on the Jaffna Peninsula, workers harvest salt that has been left behind in evaporated pools of ocean water.

In the early 1980s the industrial sector accounted for only one-fourth of the island's gross national product (the value of goods and services produced by a country in a year). State-run corporations own large-scale industries, such as the oil refinery near Colombo.

More than 20 government-owned corporations produce fertilizers, textiles, paper, leather, ceramics, chemicals, tires, oil and fats, sugar, salt, and milk. Most of these products are for local markets, although the government is trying to boost exports. Colombo is the center for most industries, but improved transportation and rural electrical facilities, as well as growing urban problems, have encouraged factories to open in the countryside.

The government has established a free-trade zone in Colombo. The zone includes advantages such as tax breaks to promote industrial growth. As a result of the new zone, Sri Lanka has increased its textile and garment production and ranks among the top 20 suppliers of finished clothing.

Energy and Transportation

Hydroelectricity provides about 90 percent of Sri Lanka's total energy needs. In the late 1980s hydroelectric installations were under construction in Laxapana and Maskeli to ensure abundant supplies of power in the near future. Part of the $2-billion Mahaweli project is a hydroelectric power plant at Victoria in the central highlands.

Sri Lanka has over 16,000 miles of roads and 900 miles of state-owned railways connecting most regions of the island. Many of the roads are tarred, but some are still narrow dirt tracks crowded with bicycles,

Products made from rubber are among Sri Lanka's manufactured items. Here, workers lift a retreaded tire from a mold.

carts, and livestock. Railways haul goods and transport people, and ferry services connect Sri Lanka with nearby India. The best roads and railways link the plantation areas to Colombo—the nation's main port.

On the local level, state-owned buses and private minibus services offer transport to local communities. In rural areas zebus or oxen pull carts, and people often travel on foot.

Sri Lankan students view the Mahaweli hydroelectric facilities at Victoria in the central highlands.

Sri Lanka operates an international airport at Katunayake, near Colombo, and has several other major airports in the country. The government-owned national airline, Air Lanka, provides domestic and international services on scheduled flights to India, Asia, and points in Europe. Air services have been improved to attract a greater share of tourists who travel to Southeast Asia.

Tourism

For decades, Sri Lanka has seen the value of developing its tourist trade. As a result, the government created the Ceylon Tourist Board in 1966 to expand and improve the nation's facilities for visitors. Guesthouses and hotels were built in all the major cities and in most towns. In the 1980s tourism brought about $1 million annually in foreign revenue to Sri Lanka.

Sri Lanka offers the visitor good communications and transport, a variety of natural scenery, a magnificent array of architectural treasures from the past, and the pageantry of an ancient culture. In addition, recreational facilities for golfing, spearfishing, skin diving, surfing, sunbathing, and mountain climbing are well developed. The large network of national parks provides the chance to see and photograph many animals in their native habitats.

Despite these attractions, the civil war between government troops and the Sri Lankan Tamil has limited the nation's appeal as a tourist spot. Indeed, since 1983 the government has advised visitors to avoid travel to the northern and eastern provinces, where much of the violence occurs.

Continuing Challenges

After over 400 years of colonial rule, Sri Lanka achieved independence without bloodshed. With fertile soil and a favorable agricultural climate, Sri Lanka national-

Photo by Drs. A. A. M. van der Heyden, Naarden, the Netherlands

Ox-drawn carts often haul wood and other goods in rural areas.

Photo by Ruthi Soudack

The Kandy perahera draws visitors from around the world to festivities that are held every summer.

Drummers are vital participants in the Buddhist celebrations at Kandy, where they also call believers to puja, or religious services, every day.

Courtesy of Ceylon Tourist Board, Colombo

Courtesy of Nathan Rabe

Elephants live in safety in several Sri Lankan national parks, including Yala and Lahugala. Ironically, many of these protected reserves have been closed to visitors in recent years because of ethnic violence on the island.

ized many of its income-producing farms after independence, while attempting to develop and broaden its range of products for both domestic and foreign markets. Its system of rural and urban medical care has produced the highest life expectancy and the lowest infant mortality in southern Asia. Yet, despite these beneficial changes, Sri Lanka has experienced serious ethnic problems in the 1980s.

The current internal conflict between government troops and Tamil guerrillas has reached neither a political nor a military solution. Indian forces—sent to protect civilians and to disarm the rebels —have become trapped in a complex ethnic dispute. Until the conflicting groups achieve civil peace, Sri Lanka's great potential for growth, stability, and prosperity remains in jeopardy.

63

Index